THE PRENUPTIAL AGREEMENT

THE PRENUPTIAL AGREEMENT

Halakhic and Pastoral Considerations

edited by
Rabbi Kenneth Auman
and Rabbi Basil Herring

A Project of The Orthodox Caucus

JASON ARONSON INC.
Northvale, New Jersey
London

This book was set in 12 pt. Antiqua by Alpha Graphics of Pittsfield, New
Hampshire.

Library of Congress Cataloging-in-Publication Data

The prenuptial agreement : halakhic and pastoral considerations /
edited by Kenneth Auman, Basil Herring.
    p.   cm.
Includes bibliographical references.
ISBN 1-56821-917-2 (alk. paper)
1. Antenuptial contracts (Jewish law) 2. Marriage—Religious
aspects—Judaism. 3. Pastoral counseling (Judaism) I. Auman,
Kenneth. II. Herring, Basil.
LAW <GENERAL Pren 1996>
296.4'44—dc20   95-48948

Manufactured in the United States of America. Jason Aronson Inc. offers
books and cassettes. For information and catalog write to Jason Aronson Inc.,
230 Livingston Street, Northvale, New Jersey 07647.

Contents

Forward

Dr. Norman Lamm
President, Yeshiva University

The term *agunah* is one which has historically
been associated with those unfortunate women
whose husbands had disappeared, or were miss-
ing for one or another reason, and who therefore
were not free to remarry. Indeed the rabbinic lit-
erature, in the codes and responsa, as well as in
the Talmud, has always been extraordinarily pre-
occupied with ameliorating the tragic fate of such
women who find themselves indefinitely and literally "anchored" to their absent spouses.

But it is only in modern times that a new phe-
nomenon has emerged: some men deliberately
inflict the status of *iggun* on their spouses, for ulterior motives, by refusing to initiate the *get* process as required by halakhah. This has become an
acute communal problem that demands redress.
As a result of the loss of authority of the community and its judicial institutions, and a concomi-

tant inability to exert uniform social sanctions upon recalcitrant husbands, the refusal to "give a *get*" has posed a particularly difficult challenge to the contemporary orthodox community, both lay and rabbinic.

Among the solutions that have been offered in recent years in addressing the complexities of the issue, the prenuptial agreement formulated with great care and precision by Rabbi Mordechai Willig has received wide support and acceptance. The Orthodox Caucus in particular is to be commended for undertaking to sponsor, underwrite, and promote the prenuptial compact, to as broad a segment of the Jewish community as possible. As part of that effort, this booklet is an important contribution to the effort to make that prenuptial contract better understood, more accessible, and easier to implement in the context of the *chuppah* and wedding preparations. It is my fervent hope that in the not too distant future, the use of the prenuptial will become *de rigeur* at *all* weddings, as an integral element of every marriage ceremony, reflecting true mutual love and respect, and social responsibility, in a shared commitment to each other and the greater glory of Torah, and to a life of *derekh eretz*–one of Jewish dignity and moral sensitivity.

Approbation

Rabbi Gedalia Dov Schwartz
Rosh Beth Din, The Beth Din of America

The use of a halakhically valid prenuptial agreement demonstrates a most practical procedure that can reduce the possible number of spouses that are prevented from receiving a *get*. In including the prenuptial agreement in the wedding plans and preparation of our couples, rabbis are challenged to display extreme sensitivity and foresight in explaining and educating both *chasan* and *kallah* in regard to its importance, while praying that the actual document will never be necessary for enforcement. The psychological factors in discussing its implementation are key components of its acceptance by the couple, and every rabbi must be prepared to deal with its discussion and use in the most delicate manner.

I have been impressed by the extraordinary efforts of Rabbi Mordechai Willig in formulating an acceptable halakhic prenuptial agreement. I have added my endorsement to this document besides those of leading rabbinic authorities in Israel and in the United States. As Rosh Beth Din of the Beth Din of America, I intend to expedite its utilization by the Beth Din and the Rabbinical Council of America.

(Signed) Rabbi Gedalia Dov Schwartz

Preface

"Hillel would say: 'Be a disciple of Aharon: love peace, pursue peace, cherish your fellows, and bring them close to the Torah.'" (*Pirkei Avot* 1:12) *Rashi*: . . . When a husband would say to his wife 'you will have no pleasure from me until you spit in the eye of the *Kohen Gadol*,' Aharon would tell that woman that he had a pain in his eye that would only be ameliorated by her spittle. For this reason, the Torah says that when Aharon died the entire house of Israel, men as well as women, grieved.

In these celebrated few words of Hillel, as expanded upon by Rashi, lie the motive and justification for this booklet. For as we confront the realities of contemporary Jewish marriage and family life, we do well to become disciples and imitators, in word and in deed, of Aharon. In the first place we should "love peace" by seeking to bring men and women together in love and devotion to each other. And then too, we should "pursue peace," cultivating domestic tranquillity to strengthen, and if necessary salvage, marriages that encounter difficulty, all too often (as in Rashi) out of a cruel spite and insensitivity, on the part of one spouse. But sometimes, sadly, it happens that marriages fail, and cannot be resuscitated, even by an Aharon. It is then that, like Aharon of old, we should "cherish our fellows," those individuals who are in real need of our personal and communal intercession, to care for their woes and protect their vulnerabilities. Then, and only then, can we feel with justification that we have not distanced them, or our contemporaries, from the Torah, but to the contrary, will have brought them and the larger community to a more profound and compelling appreciation of the moral and spiritual resources of our precious Torah and its halakhic framework.

The prenuptial agreement that is the core of this slim volume, is a sincere, and we believe, effective, attempt to follow in the footsteps of Aharon. It seeks to prevent the occurrence of *iggun*, which result when recalcitrant husbands refuse to grant their wives a *get*, for ulterior motive, even when it is clear that their marriage cannot be salvaged. The inability to deal effectively with this problem, given contemporary social and cultural trends and realities, has been a mark of ignominy upon the Torah community for many years. But thanks to this prenuptial, as formulated by Rabbi Mordechai Willig, under the auspices of the Orthodox Caucus, there is genuine hope that future cases of *iggun* can be significantly diminished, if not avoided altogether. But in truth this will only happen when most, if not all, new marriages will incorporate the prenuptial as a *sine qua non* preceding every ceremony, thus avoiding to the maximum degree possible any doubts as to the intentions of any particular spouse-to-be.

For this reason, this booklet is presented to the broader Jewish community. Laymen as well as rabbis will hereby have the texts and supporting material easily available to them, so as to facilitate the broadest possible utilization of the prenuptial. The text itself is also available for purchase separately, in an attractive format more esthetically conducive to actual implementation prior to the wedding ceremony itself. That text, attractively packaged together with other marriage documents such as the *tena'im* and *ketubah*, can be purchased through the Rabbinical Council of America, and through bookstores that stock general Judaica items.

We are indebted to the various authors and publishers who have allowed us to present this material in the present form. And we are indebted to the Orthodox Caucus for its unqualified and consistent support of the prenuptial agreement itself, including its underwriting of the costs of publication of this volume.

As with Hillel, may our combined efforts bring a greater measure of justice to every Jew, man and woman, within marriage and beyond. And may they bring abiding honor and respect for the creative vitality of our precious halakhic legacy, embodied in a life faithful to Torah and *mitzvah*, today as always.

 Rabbi Kenneth Auman
 Rabbi Basil Herring
 Cheshvan 5756 / November 1995

I
BACKGROUND OF THE PRENUPTIAL

On the Compelling Need for an Effective Prenuptial Agreement

Rabbi Saul J. Berman

Many of my rabbinic colleagues have told me that they are reluctant to use a prenuptial agreement related to assurance of issuance of a *get* upon dissolution of the marriage by civil divorce. I am deeply dismayed by this reluctance, albeit I have some understanding of why such reticence exists. Why is a prenuptial agreement necessary?

The inability of Jewish courts in the United States to compel a husband to issue a *get* to his wife, because of lack of jurisdiction and enforcement powers, has resulted in a powerful advantage held by the husband. Unfortunately, some husbands, often cruelly and unethically advised to do so by their attorneys, choose to exploit this advantage by using the issuance of the *get* as lever-

Reprinted with permission from *Rabbinics Today,* 2:3, December 1993

age for the achievement of other purposes, such as monetary extortion or reordering child custody arrangements.

Great Jewish minds have devoted not insignificant amounts of energy to produce a solution to this problem. As the dust settles after almost forty years of deliberation and debate, both Orthodoxy and the Conservative movement have elected a common approach, albeit in differing frameworks. The Conservative movement, under the guidance of the late Rabbi Saul Lieberman, added a clause to the *ketubah* which would make an order of a rabbinic court enforceable in civil courts in the manner of binding arbitration.

Orthodoxy, with great fanfare rejected this particular device, but affirmed the approach of using the American civil courts as the means of resolving this problem. Thus, Agudath Israel, under the leadership of their *Mo'etzet Gedolei HaTorah*, went the legislative route and successfully supported the passage of the *Get* Statute in the State of New York. The Rabbinical Council of America, under the leadership of the late Rav Yosef Dov Ha-Levi Soloveitchik, elected rather the use of a prenuptial agreement which would bind the parties through their own prior consent to be subjected to significant financial loss through their failure to issue a *get* in a timely fashion. The struggle within Orthodoxy to fine tune the prenuptial agreement into a document capable of being assented to by virtually all Torah circles, has taken almost fifteen years, and has left many sacrificed *agunot* by the wayside of life during the struggle. This has been an infuriating and almost intolerable time for sensitive Orthodox Jews to live through. But it now appears, finally, that a document having the consensus of most Orthodox *halakhic* leaders is truly at hand.

Rabbi Mordechai Willig, of Yeshiva University, has, with the timeless strength of great Jewish leaders, shepherded through the hands and hearts of the leadership of the *halakhic* community, a new prenuptial document. The documents have been approved for use by Ashkenazic and Sephardic scholars in Israel, by a very diverse set of Haredi and American Orthodox *poskim* here in the United States. Whether one takes the attitude of "it's about time," or of "patience has finally been rewarded," the time seems now to be at hand for the universal Orthodox adoption of the use of these documents.

The next and most crucial step in the resolution of this problem now lies in the power of the rabbinate. If we, all of us together, can interpret the importance of, and insist on the use of, these documents at every Jewish marriage, then we will rid Jewish society of this scourge which now afflicts our moral condition as a people. This is one time when our united energies are essential. Only when every Jewish couple has such a document will those who will need it be protected.

I understand the sense of reluctance which many rabbis have about discussing divorce and possible extortion in the midst of premarital counselling. Yet, is not the entire *ketubah* precisely a contract in contemplation of divorce or death of the husband? And people hang illustrated texts of the *ketubah* over their beds! The point is that the very universality of the *ketubah* allows people to accept it without feeling that they are making a negative statement about the expected longevity of their marriage. The same can eventually be true of these prenuptial documents.

What, I believe, will ease the process of use of these documents is their use in place of the traditional *tena'im*, which are now in any case almost always used only to increase the number of honors available for distribution at the wedding. We ought also transfer over to these new *tena'im* the custom of the active presence of the mothers, either still breaking a plate, or performing some other act indicating the protective responsibility of mothers.

As rabbis, we only rarely have the opportunity to shape a new and universal Jewish practice while simultaneously helping to prevent Jewish immorality. Such a joint opportunity is now before us. Our creativity can mold the practice, our capacity as teachers and leaders will be tested in the process of convincing this coming first generation of users to be comfortable with the process, and our ethical vigor will leave a lasting mark on all future generations of Jews.

The Modern Day *Agunah*: In Retrospect and Prospect

Rabbi Avraham Weiss

The most serious challenge facing Jewish women today, is the modern day *agunah*, women whose marriages have failed, but who cannot obtain a *get* from their husband.[1] For even if their marriage is dissolved by civil authorities, under Jewish law the couple remains married and unable to enter into a new marriage, leaving married Jewish women exposed and endangered to years of anguish and blackmail.

HISTORICAL OVERVIEW[2]

When considering the history of *get*, it becomes clear that the modern *agunah* problem is one born of the American Jewish experience.

---

1. While such issues as women in prayer and women in Talmud Torah have precipitated much discussion, it is the *agunah* problem that is far more overbearing, as it prevents women from marrying and continuing their personal lives. According to a paper published some years ago by an organization called *Agunah*, "there are an estimated 3000, to 6000 *agunot* in the U.S. and Israel."

The Torah states "and he shall write her a bill of divorce and place it in her hands" (Deut. 24:1). In other words, the giving of a *get* is the husband's exclusive domain. He and only he can initiate divorce and he may effect divorce unilaterally. While it is difficult to pinpoint why the Torah so decreed, it could be suggested that since women in biblical times found it difficult and even impossible to fend for themselves socio-economically, they would under no circumstances desire a *get*.[3] The Torah reflects this reality by providing that the husband give a *get* as the wife would never initiate such a proceeding.

This unilateral right of the husband to divorce his wife was limited by the advent of the *ketubah* (marital contract)[4] which details the many obligations that a husband has to his wife, including an amount of money that his wife would receive in case of divorce. In this way, a husband's absolute power to divorce his wife was severely restricted. This financial obligation would make him think twice before indiscriminately giving a *get* to his wife; thus the *ketubah* served as a deterrent to the unilateral divorce.

The unilateral power of the husband to give the *get* disappeared in its entirety a thousand years

2. Many thanks to Rabbi Shlomo Riskin, from whom I first heard the framework of this historical overview. See his excellent book, *Women and Jewish Divorce*, (New Jersey: Ktav, 1978).

3. See Resh Lakish's comment in *Kiddushin* 41a, "A woman would rather live with grief than live alone." There is, however, evidence that even in Biblical times, some women were able to fend for themselves.

4. Some suggest that the *ketuba* goes back to biblical times. Others believe that it was instituted by Rabbi Shimon ben Shetach in 40 B.C.E.

ago when Rabbenu Gershom declared that a *get*
could not be given without the wife's consent. If
the *ketubah* made it difficult for a husband to unilaterally divorce his wife, Rabbenu Gershom ob-
viated that unilateral power in its entirety. The *get*
became a bilateral process rather than a unilateral
one.

With time, the *get* process entered yet a different stage, a stage in which women could initiate a *get*. In the middle ages, for example, cen-
tral communities in Europe were governed by the
Va'ad Arba Aratzot, the committee of the four
major Jewish population centers. Jews there had
their own political sovereignty and judicial au-
tonomy. In such a setting, the courts ruled with
an iron hand and their decisions had to be fol-
lowed. Given the fact that mobility was difficult,
and, moreover, the relationship between these
respective Jewish communities was sound, few
people could escape a decision not in their favor.
In this situation a woman could start the divorce
proceedings by going to a *bet din* and registering
complaints against her husband.[5] If the *bet din*
found her claims reason enough for divorce, it
was powerful enough to order the husband to
give the *get* to his wife.[6] While the *get* was still
physically given by husband to wife, it was effec-

---

5. The ability of women to initiate the *get* goes back to Tannaitic
times. See *Mishnah Ketabot* 7:10.

6. Of course, if a secular court coerces a husband to give the *get*,
the *get* is invalid. However, if the secular court coerces a husband to follow the decree of the *bet din*, the *get* is valid. see *Mishnah Gittin* 9:8;
Rambam, *Code*, Laws of Divorce 2:20; and *Shulchan Arukh Even
ha-Ezer* 134.5, 8, 9.

tively taken out of the husband's exclusive domain and placed into the domain of the *bet din*. As long as the *bet din* was strong enough, the *agunah* problem was resolved.

Of course, the situation in the United States at this time is different. Here, because of the principle of separation of Church and State, a *bet din* has no legal power to implement its decisions. In this sense, American Jews are weaker than their counterparts who lived in Babylonia or medieval Europe. In the United States, as in other places in the exile, a husband can flout the demands of the *bet din* and simply refuse to give his wife a *get*.

This has created a situation where a husband could blackmail his wife by demanding exorbitant sums of money or custody of their child(ren) before giving his wife a *get*, even when the *bet din* believes the *get* should be issued.

SOLUTIONS

In the past, several approaches have been suggested to solve the *agunah* problem. Many of the suggestions have been rejected by the rabbinate.

While the purpose of this paper is not to analyze what constitutes a forced *get*, note Rambam, Code, Laws of Divorce 2:20. There, Rambam the arch rationalist, resorts to a mystical argument when discussing the issue of *kefiyah* (forced *get*). He argues that every Jew possesses a higher will and desires to do the right thing. Therefore, if the *bet din* concludes that a wife's claim for divorce is justified, the *bet din* would merely be forcing the husband to do that which he in truth wants to do, i.e., give the *get*.

For example, in the late 19th century, Rabbi Michael Weil of Paris suggested that all marriages be made conditional. At the marriage ceremony, the groom would say to his bride "Behold, you are wed to me; however, if the judges of the state will divorce us and I not give you a Jewish divorce, this marriage will be retroactively invalid."[7] The proposal was rejected by the European rabbinate. In 1967 Rabbi Eliezer Berkovits of Skokie IL, attempted to reopen the issue of conditional marriage. It too was rejected. The rejection, in no small measure, had to do with the belief that a conditional marriage would undercut what should be the unconditional commitment between husband and wife.[8]

In 1954, Professor Saul Lieberman of the Conservative movement's Jewish Theological Seminary introduced a new clause to the Conservative *ketubah*. In it, bride and groom agree that the Rabbinical Assembly *bet din* will arbitrate in case of divorce. Thus the husband would be obliged to give his wife a *get* if the *bet din so* decreed. In the event he refused, the new stipulation provided that the *bet din* would "impose such terms of compensation as it might see fit, for failure to respond to its summons to carry out its decision." Professor Lieberman maintained that the civil courts could enforce this agreement.

---

7. Quoted by Rabbi Moshe Meiselman, *Jewish Women in Jewish Law.* New York: Ktav Publishing House, 1978, p. 104.

8. See Rabbi Eliezer Berkovits, in *Tnai be-Nisuin ve-Get* (1967). See Rabbi Meiselman's volume for a summary of this proposal, pp. 104-108.

The Lieberman proposal was rejected by the Orthodox rabbinate. The latter argued that an agreement to pay a non-specified amount of money is an *asmakhta*, and not halakhically valid.[9] Moreover, constitutional questions were raised as to whether the civil courts could enforce the *ketubah* which many viewed as a religious document.[10]

Today, however, there have emerged three viable halakhic options.

A. SANCTIONS

One is to impose communal sanctions—both social and financial—on the recalcitrant party. In 1979 Rabbi Saul Berman and I drafted such a proposal and submitted it to the Rabbinical Council of America's Commission on Divorce. It included announcing the recalcitrant party's name every Shabbat morning in synagogue, publishing the recalcitrant party's name in the Anglo-Jewish press and general newspapers, and calling upon members of the community to avoid social and economic relations with such persons. For the past

---

9. See Rabbi Norman Lamm, "Recent Additions to the Ketuba," Tradition 2, 1 (Fall 1959) pp. 93-119. In his words: "the essential fault of the Conservative proposal ... is its extremely indeterminate nature, a vagueness which Jewish law cannot tolerate as the proper basis for legal negotiation."

10. Some experts maintain the *ketubah is* a personal contract between two people which the civil courts can uphold. See Irwin H. Haut, *Divorce in Jewish Law and Life,* New York: Sepher-Hermon Press, 1983, pp. 81-82.

fifteen years it has been my practice to ban recalcitrant spouses from entering our synagogue.

Rabbi Berman and I also suggested that the RCA look into the legality of placing regular telephone calls at all hours of the day or night to the recalcitrant's home or business, using direct and repeated contact with employer and/or business associates to explain the gravity of the moral turpitude involved, picketing the recalcitrant's home or place of business, and systematically interfering with the earning capacity of the recalcitrant party. By 1994 both the RCA and OU had finally adopted a resolution calling on synagogues to use such sanctions.

Writing on the subject of sanctions, Rabbi Joseph Grunblatt in the RCA's *Family and Marriage Newsletter* (Spring 1979), declared "The least we can do is to recite every Shabbat morning a curse against those who make others suffer, just as we recite a blessing for those who work for the needs of the community."

B. CIVIL LEGAL SYSTEM

A second approach is to solve the problem through the civil legal system. An example is the New York State *Get* Law, which says that the plaintiff must remove all barriers that would prevent his spouse's remarriage before a civil divorce could be granted. There is no issue of *kefiyah* (forced *get*) in the original New York *Get* Law, since the civil court was only acting to withhold a civil benefit, which is of no recognized religious value.

The 1992 amendment to the New York *Get* Law has raised *kefiyah* problems because, as I understand it, it empowers the judge to take into account the husband's refusal to issue a *get,* in the judicial determination of the equitable distribution of the marriage property. Here, Rabbi Saul Berman has argued that this could constitute *kefiyah* as there is direct monetary pressure placed upon the husband to influence him to issue a *get.*

C. PRENUPTIAL AGREEMENT[11]

A third approach has every bride and groom sign a prenuptial agreement. Such an agreement was drafted in the early 1980's by the RCA's Commission on Divorce chaired by Rabbi Abner Weiss. The agreement states that bride and groom agree that, in case of dissolution of the marriage by either divorce or annulment, each party consents to a *get,* that is, the husband agrees to issue the *get,* and the wife agrees to accept it. There is recognition in the agreement that the refusal of either party to give

---

11. Rabbi Moshe Tendler is of the opinion that the *ketubah* itself can resolve much of the *agunah* problem, without resorting to a separate prenuptial agreement. To this end he has produced a document detailing the husband's obligation to his wife as found in the *ketubah* itself. The document is signed when the *ketubah is* witnessed. It is Rabbi Tendler's position that such a document constitutes real financial pressure on a recalcitrant husband. There are no new penalties, hence no problem of a *get me'useh (forced get.)* Furthermore there is no church-state dilemma, because the contract does not compel any religious act. The parties to the *ketubah* merely agree that the contact is abrogated once the specific act is performed.

or receive the *get* results in actual damage to the party then kept unable to remarry against his or her will. Compensation for that damage is agreed to in advance by a specified *per diem* sum. There is no *kefiyah* as the payment is not a penalty to compel the husband to give the *get,* but rather a payment to compensate his wife for the damages imposed on her. Or, if the situation is the reverse, and it is the wife who refuses to receive the *get*, she compensates him for the damages she has imposed on him.

The prenuptial agreement drafted by Rabbi Mordechai Willig is different. It stipulates that for every day that husband and wife are separated, even prior to divorce, the wife is entitled to demand of her husband a specified *per diem* sum for her support.[12] Both husband and wife agree prenuptially to come before a previously designated *bet din* to arbitrate the *get*. Should the wife refuse to appear before the court or fail to abide by the court's decision, the husband's financial obligation is terminated.

This prenuptial agreement has been approved by Rabbi Ovadiah Yosef, former Sephardic Chief Rabbi of Israel, and Rabbi Zalman Nechemiah

---

[12]The *ketubah* obligation of the husband to sustain his wife in marriage only applies when husband and wife live together. If they are apart even prior to divorce, the wife must demonstrate that their separation is her husband's fault in order to continue receiving financial support. In the prenuptial agreement drafted by Rabbi Willig, the husband undertakes an independent support obligation which takes effect only in the event of separation.

Goldberg, who serves on the Bet Din of Jerusalem. The agreement has also been approved by the RCA, which urges its members to use it. The support that this document has received from across the Orthodox rabbinic spectrum makes it an extraordinary breakthrough.[13]

IMPORTANCE OF THE PRENUPTIAL

From my perspective, it would be irresponsible for any rabbi to perform a wedding without a prenuptial agreement having been signed. This has been my policy since 1984 and indeed, my own children have signed the prenuptial agreement.

In fact, it would be wise for our community to begin a campaign to have married couples similarly sign a postnuptial agreement. Not only would this be important for married couples, but it would also teach our children by example how crucial this document is.

So important is the prenuptial agreement, that it and the larger issue of *agunah* should be part of yeshiva curricula, in lower schools, high schools and colleges. I've devoted segments of courses in my classes at Stern College, Yeshiva University, to teach this issue.

And to underscore how critical it is to confront

---

13. There are numerous other prenuptial agreements that have been drafted. See David Joseph Mescheloff, "The Problem of the Forced Jewish Divorce and Prenuptial Agreements as a Solution to the Problem of Abandoned Wives," MA Thesis, Bar Ilan University, 1994.

the *agunah* problem head-on, a special prayer for *agunot* should be recited in synagogue to sensitize our community to the *agunah* horror and our responsibility to resolve the issue.

A FINAL WORD

There are many who ask "how can a rabbi insist that bride and groom, so deeply in love, sign a prenuptial agreement which deals with divorce?" The truth is that bride and groom already commit themselves to the *ketubah* which is primarily an alimony and insurance policy. As it is impossible for rabbis to perform a wedding without a *ketubah* despite the fact that it deals with marriage termination, so should the collective rabbinate declare that no marriage will be performed without a prenuptial agreement.

Moreover, it is the rabbi's sacred task to tell and teach each bride and groom that a test of love is how one prepares when in control, for those moments when one is not in control.

The Talmud notes that God gathers the tears of those who divorce.[14] Divorce is painful enough. In recent years, with the surfacing of many *agunot,* it has become more painful. Perhaps, more than most of my colleagues, I've seen the suffering of many *agunot.* This is because over the past 25 years, I've taught Torah to thousands of students at Stern College. Almost everywhere I go in my

---

14. See *Gittin* 90b

travels, a former student approaches me to share her *agunah* plight.

Too often we've heard the *agunah* cry out "if only I had signed the prenuptial agreement." It's a cry we should all heed.

Approbations of the Prenuptial Text

Rashei Bet Din

(translated, in alphabetical order)

MEMBER, BET DIN OF JERUSALEM, RABBI ZALMAN NECHEMIAH GOLDBERG

(Signed) Rabbi Zalman Nechemiah Goldberg

ROSH BET DIN, IGGUD HA-RABBONIM, RABBI YITZCHOK LIEBES

I too join and concur with this text.
(Signed) Rabbi Yitzchok Liebes

THE RISHON LE'TZION, RABBI OVADIAH YOSEF

28 Shvat 5752
I concur with the above-mentioned proposal
(Signed) Ovadiah Yosef

MEMBER OF THE BET DIN OF TEL AVIV, RABBI CHAIM G. ZIMBALIST

I hereby join with the outstanding rabbinic authorities who have agreed to the above text. (Signed) Rabbi Chaim G. Zimbalist

Resolutions of the Rabbinical Council of America

Adopted in June 1993

IN THE MATTER
OF PRENUPTIAL AGREEMENTS

I. Whereas it was clearly the desire of God that couples live together in peace and harmony, in love and devotion all of their lives, so that strong marriages could serve as the heart of a strong Jewish community; but

Whereas the Torah recognized that some marriages could not be sustained and therefore provided procedures for the termination of those marriages, so that husband and wife could then be freed to create new and stronger marriages; but

Whereas in some unfortunate instances husbands or wives, for reasons of spite or venality, refuse to cooperate with the appropriate instructions of a *bet din* regarding the termination of their marriages with a *get*, thereby preventing the spouse from rebuilding family life.

II. Therefore, be it resolved that every member of the Rabbinical Council of America will utilize prenuptial agreements, which will aid in our community's efforts to guarantee that the *get* will not be used as a negotiating tool in divorce procedures. We realize that there are several prenuptial agreements and many may raise halakhic or legal difficulties. We, therefore, call upon the Executive Committee of the Rabbinical Council of America to disseminate a list of approved prenuptial agreements with procedures of implementation to the chaverim. All prenuptial agreements must be approved by the Rabbinical Council of America's *bet din*. To this date only Rabbi Willig's prenuptial agreement has been accepted and this document will be distributed immediately to the Rabbinical Council of America members.

ADOPTED IN JUNE 1994
REAFFIRMING THE ENDORSEMENT OF PRENUPTIAL AGREEMENTS

. . . Therefore be it resolved that the RCA reiterates the importance of using the prenuptial agreement as per the 1993 resolution, so as to guarantee that the *get* will not be used as a negotiating tool in divorce procedures.

The RCA members will attempt to disseminate amongst our Orthodox colleagues and lay people via the mediums of Shabbat sermons, synagogue bulletins, and other forums during the month of Cheshvan, the importance of the prenuptial agreement.

Endorsements from the Pulpit Rabbinate

"Couples are quite responsive to the need for a prenuptial agreement. Brides and grooms find this to be a thoughtful document which serves an important need within the Jewish community. Since this is a way of relieving the *agunah* problem, it seems to me that each rabbi should sense a moral obligation to the suffering of even one couple, then the entire enterprise is worthwhile."

Rabbi Marc D. Angel
New York, NY

"I have used Rabbi Willig's prenuptial agreement on three different occasions in the last year with great acceptability. The ease of language and the sense of mutual concern put the couples at ease regarding such a tense issue."

Rabbi Moshe Bomzer
Albany, NY

"In my younger years, I was part of the community that was torn apart over a *get* controversy. At that time, I decided that if ever a mechanism were found to avoid such human tragedy, I would become an advocate for it. Rabbi Willig's prenuptial agreement which I require for any couple whose marriage I perform, serves that purpose admirably. Combining remarkable erudition with an ability to translate scholarly learning into pragmatic reality, this device goes a long way to ensuring that the tragedy of women unable to free themselves once a marriage has irretrievably broken down, can be avoided."

Rabbi Barry Freundel
Washington, D.C.

"I have used the prenuptial agreement authored by Rabbi Mordechai Willig when performing marriages over these past few years. This agreement, carefully crafted and constructed, offers a practical way to address the painful problem of potential *agunot* in our community. With the proper approach, the prenuptial agreement is readily accepted by individuals preparing for marriage. I certainly encourage its use."

Rabbi Shmuel Goldin
Engelwood, NJ

"Ever since Rabbi Willig published the agreement I have insisted on its use at every wedding at which I officiate. It has helped immeasurably in addressing the concerns that families have about the possibility of divorce, and how we can ensure that a *get* will be issued in a timely fashion. This document, endorsed by the major halakhic authorities, is an asset for the Orthodox rabbinate."

Rabbi Elazar R. Muskin
Los Angeles, CA

"Before settling on the Willig prenuptial agreement as the one I share with brides and grooms, I investigated others. I believe that Rabbi Willig has produced a document that is not only halakhically acceptable but can also be easily explained to brides and grooms."

Rabbi Milton H. Polin
Brooklyn, NY

"I have found Rabbi Willig's agreement to be innovative within the framework of halakhah. The fruits of his intellectual creativity should greatly reduce the incidence of abuse of the *get* process which all too frequently plagues our community."

Rabbi Steven Pruzansky
Teaneck, NJ

"The prenuptial agreement penned by Rabbi Willig is an invaluable *hatzaloh purtoh* during these turbulent times . . . . . . I have deliberately discussed its importance with every *choson* and *kallah,* and urge its usage to stem the tragic tide of *agunos.*"

Rabbi Yaakov Sprung
North Miami Beach, FL

"Rabbi Willig's halakhic erudition has brought forth a very important document which serves to bring peace of mind to a Jewish couple and in particular to Jewish women, before entering into the holy covenant of marriage. I have found the use of the prenuptial agreement a terrific springboard into discussing the sanctity of marriage from a Jewish point of view."

Rabbi Ronald L. Schwarzberg,
Highland Park, NJ

"Rabbi Willig's prenuptial document, which has the halakhic support of leading *poskim*, is to be commended for usage by all. It is clear that its acceptance and practice will contribute to a lessening of real and potential abuses and predicaments during divorce proceeding."

Rabbi Moshe J. Yeres
Wilkes-Barre, PA

II
HALAKHIC AND LEGAL CONSIDERATIONS

The Halakhic Sources and Background of the Prenuptial

Rabbi Mordechai Willig

I. PREFACE

The idea of a prenuptial agreement which encourages the parties to appear before a *bet din* in the unfortunate event of marital strain or break-up is not new. Over 300 years ago, the *Nachalat Shiva* included such a provision in his classic collection of documents, incorporating it into the standard *tena'im* conditions entered into before marriage.[1] The author of the *Nachalat Shiva*, a disciple of the *Taz*, cited authorities who attribute this provision to *Takanot Shum*, instituted in Germany over 500 years ago.[2] Today's *poskim* differ on the specifics of the monetary obligation which should be em-

---

1. *Nachalat Shiva*, ch. 9
2. Ibid. Sub-paragraph 14

ployed in such an agreement. Some prefer a conditional obligation of support in the event of marital separation, similar to the form proposed by the *Nachalat Shiva*.[3] Others feel that an unconditional obligation running from the date of the marriage should be prepared. The *poskim* also disagree about the size of the obligation.[4]

The primary obstacle to the widespread use of prenuptial agreements appears to be the reluctance of *rabbanim* to introduce innovations to the institution of marriage. Thus, there is even a widespread reluctance to employ a simple arbitration agreement, referring future marital disputes to a particular *bet din*, an agreement which is *halakhically* noncontroversial.[5] Such an agreement could avoid the frequent bitter battles over which *bet din* should hear a particular dispute. A legally binding arbitration agreement would also solve the problems of one party applying to the secular courts to gain an advantage over the other in marital disputes.

The precedent of centuries ago should allay the fears of *rabbanim* concerning innovation. In practice, the need for a prenuptial agreement is greater now, when there is no centralized *bet din* system, than it was in the *Nachalat Shiva*'s time. Moreover, the secular courts are no longer systematically hostile to Jews and are now a practical option for unhappy couples. Finally, the role of *bet*

---

3. *Moriah,* Iyyar 5748, quoting Rabbi Zalman Nechemiah Goldberg

4. See Rabbi J. David Bleich, *Or ha-Mizra*, Tishri 5750.

5. Rabbi Moshe Feinstein, *Iggerot Moshe, Even ha-Ezer* 4:107

din in restoring marital harmony (*shalom bayit*) to which the *Nachalat Shiva* also refers, should not be ignored at a time of high divorce rates.

Self interest should also prompt *rabbanim* to reconsider their reluctance to use a prenuptial agreement. The congregational rabbi is often at the center of a controversy over which *bet din* will consider a case of marital breakup. The problem of the recalcitrant spouse is also a source of anguish for the rabbi, who shares the pain of *iggun* and is frustrated by, and all too frequently attacked for, his inability to solve it.

The two forms directly address and ameliorate all of these problems, even if they cannot solve all of them once and for all. If they are widely used, they will substantially diminish the occurrence of *iggun* and facilitate the *halakhically* acceptable adjudication and resolution of marital strife cases in general.

II. ARBITRATION AGREEMENT

There are two separate documents to be executed by the parties. The first of these is an arbitration agreement, which binds the parties to accept rabbinic arbitration of serious marital disputes. It is signed by both the future husband and wife and is a legally enforceable arbitration agreement. The gist of the agreement is the binding acceptance of rabbinic arbitration before a *bet din* of marital disputes when the husband and wife are not living together.

The agreement offers the parties a choice of a *bet din*. If the officiating rabbi prefers a particular *bet din*, it is prudent to include its name in the printed text of the agreement when it is presented to the soon-to-be-married couple. If the name is left blank, the chances of one or both parties objecting to the rabbi's oral suggestion is likely increased. If no *bet din* is specified in the agreement, the parties may not be able to agree later on any *bet din* when tensions between them are high, creating an additional source of conflict. If presented with a standard form, the parties are more likely to accept the rabbi's preference. If the rabbi feels that in a given case a different *bet din* is more appropriate, this change should better be made in the original, printed form.

Rabbanim should research carefully the decisions and practices of a *bet din* before suggesting it to the parties. If the parties question the rabbi's choice, he must be able to defend it properly. If the parties insist on a different *bet din* than the one suggested by the rabbi, the form must be revised to reflect their choice. If the parties cannot agree, the form should state that the parties agree to submit to arbitration by any one of several *batei din*, which should then be specified, or a *bet din* of *zabla* (in which each party picks a rabbinic judge, and these two judges picks a third).

The second option concerns the scope of the *bet din*'s authority. The authority of the *bet din* may be limited to the *get*, the *ketubah* and the *tena'im*. See paragraph 3(a) of the Arbitration Agreement. If the parties agree, the document may include other issues in the arbitration agreement (*e.g.*, support, custody, or the division of property.) See paragraphs 3b,3c, and 3d. Each of these three clauses is optional, to be included or excluded by mutual consent, when signing the agreement. Rabbis should know, however, that in no, or almost no, state of the U.S. will the secular courts defer to a *bet din* on matters of child custody. An agreement to arbitrate such disputes may give rise to expectations which cannot later be fulfilled.

Some women or their attorneys will object to the inclusion of monetary disputes (e.g., property settlements, alimony, child support) in the arbitration agreement, for the current secular laws of equitable distribution and maintenance or community property will generally result in larger financial settlements for women than does enforcing the provisions of the standard *ketubah*. *Halakhically*, however, resolutions of marital property disputes are within the jurisdiction of a *bet din*, unless *bet din* permits the parties to resolve them in court.

It does not follow from the fact that *bet din* is the appropriate tribunal to hear marital property disputes that the parties cannot themselves agree to financial arrangements other than those prescribed by the *halakhah* in the absence of an agreement. If both parties agree in advance that *bet din* should decide their financial affairs according to a specified law of a designated secular jurisdiction, the *bet din* should do so. We have included an optional agreement (see paragraph 3(d)) which requires the use of equitable distribution, the most commonly used form of property division in divorce cases. Acceptance of an agreement about financial matters is surely preferable to the wholesale exclusion of monetary disputes from the arbitration agreement which will result in their resolution by the secular courts.

III. HUSBAND'S OBLIGATION

The second document details the husband's obligation of support in the event that the couple are living apart from one another. The only option in this agreement is the sum allotted for daily support. The rabbi may prefer a fixed sum, *e.g.*, $100.00 a day, which is to be adjusted annually to reflect changes in the specified Consumer Price Index, or he may adjust the initial sum based on the financial status of the parties, a sum which again will be adjusted annually for changes in the specified Consumer Price Index. In either case, it is wise to pre-print the sum only if a dispute over the amount is anticipated. Otherwise, it is legally and *halachically* appropriate to have the sum inserted later, but before the parties sign the document, to insure that the groom realizes the nature and size of the obligation he is accepting.

Some may prefer to omit the obligation entirely, for halachic or pragmatic reasons. A prospective husband may refuse to accept this support obligation, but be willing to accept the arbitration agreement. If so, and efforts at persuading him to accept this obligation fail, he should still be encouraged to sign the arbitration agreement. If the husband later refuses to abide by the decision of the rabbinic arbitrators (*bet din*) reached either with his participation or after his default, the *bet din*'s judgment would be enforceable in the secular courts as an arbitrator's decision.

Still, there is a substantial advantage if the support obligation is accepted. The presence of an independent financial liability will typically enable the *bet din* to expedite resolution of all marital disputes, either to effect reconciliation or to terminate the marriage in a *halakhically* acceptable way. A husband is less likely to ignore a *bet din* when an obligation of a specific sum of support accrues automatically than when the *bet din* must decide whether to impose one and what its amount should be.

The support obligation is entered into when the groom executes *kinyan sudar* by taking hold of a utensil (*e.g.*, a handkerchief) belonging to the rabbi. The document should then be signed by the groom and two kosher witnesses.

A Legal Guide to the Prenuptial Agreement for Couples about to Be Married

Marc D. Stern

It no doubt seems odd to be presented with agreements dealing with the possibility of divorce in the
weeks prior to a wedding. Surely, at a time when
two people are deeply in love and are planning a
wedding, divorce seems totally beyond the realm
of the possible. The answer lies not in any suspi-
cion that any particular couple's marriage will end
in divorce. In the Orthodox community, divorce
is fortunately far less common than it is in the
general community. Unfortunately, it is not so rare
that the risk of divorce can be discounted entirely.
More to the point, the rate of divorce is increasing
even in the Orthodox community, and what is true
today may not be true ten or fifteen years from
now.

   Like a disability insurance policy, one hopes
never to have recourse to agreements concerning
divorce. But if, God forbid, one does become dis-

abled, having a disability insurance policy can be of great value. So too, these agreements concerning the details of a divorce can be of great help in making an unpleasant experience less unpleasant. They will also insure that the bitterness of some divorces does not become the occasion for blackmail under the guise of religion. There is another reason to sign these agreements. Each couple which signs the agreement indicates that it believes that religious blackmail has no place in the Jewish community. The very act of signing these agreements is a protest against, and repudiation of, religious blackmail. Even if a couple never needs to use these agreements their acceptance is a tangible victory in the battle on this issue.

A very small percentage of divorces become so bitter that the parties, or one of them, will do almost anything to spite the other party. In the Orthodox community, this sometimes results in either the husband withholding a *get*, the wife refusing to accept it, or either or both parties simply refusing to respond to a summons by the other spouse to attend the *bet din*. Jewish law requires that a marriage be terminated by a *get* which must be voluntarily given by the husband, and voluntarily accepted by the wife. The refusal of either party to give or accept a *get* can leave the other spouse stranded, unable to remarry. The consequence of this state of affairs is worse for the wife, since if she remarries without a *get* the child is illegitimate.

The two agreements are designed to be acceptable under Jewish law, and legally enforceable in the civil courts. These are not just meaningless pieces of paper. They are as important as any prenuptial agreement or any other contract. They are fully enforceable and legally binding.Both bride and groom should read these agreements carefully, and may want to consult their own attorney about these documents.

ARBITRATION AGREEMENT

The first of these agreements is an arbitration agreement. It is signed by both parties, and binds each of them to appear before a *bet din* which is empowered to decide all issues concerning a *get*. The rabbi will suggest a *bet din*, but the parties may if they wish insist on their own *bet din*. Generally, it is preferable to designate a particular organizational *bet din* (e.g., Beth Din of America, Agudas Ha-Rabbonim, etc.)

There is yet another potentially important option couples will want to consider. The current practice with regard to the *ketubah* is to provide for a fixed payment upon the death of the husband or the couple's divorce. At other times in Jewish history, it was the practice to vary these amounts based on the financial status of the parties as of the time of marriage. Moreover, within certain broad limits, Jewish law recognizes the right of the parties to restructure their marital financial arrangements to depart from standard practice. In contrast to the current halakhic practice, all states today apply some sort of scheme which apportions the property between the spouses based on their respective financial contribution to the marriage. These are known as either equitable distribution or community property schemes. Although the details vary from State to State, in practice these schemes are likely to result in a greater allocation to the wife upon divorce than does the standard *ketubah*, particularly if the wife works, and earns a substantial income. The agreement (Section 3(d)) allows the husband and the wife to agree to require the *bet din* to settle their financial arrangements under their state's equitable distribution scheme as it exists on the date of the agreement.

HUSBAND'S SUPPORT OBLIGATION

The second agreement is signed only by the husband-to-be, in return, as it were, for the future wife's agreement to marry him. It obligates him to pay his wife a daily amount for support per day. This amount will be adjusted annually for inflation. The obligation is triggered only if the parties are living apart, and ceases when the husband responds to a summons by the *bet din* or asks the *bet din* to decide the parties' marital dispute. This agreement is designed to deny to the husband any economic benefit from the too-common tactic of refusing to give a *get* unless a large sum is paid to the husband by the wife or her family. On the other hand, by stopping the obligation with the refusal of the wife to honor a summons to *bet din*, the agreement avoids any possible unfairness to the husband. In theory, these support and arbitration agreements are independent of one another. But they were designed to be applied together and will be most effective in reducing or eliminating the problem of *agunah* if all couples sign both. The choice, however, must be made by each couple in consultation with their rabbi.

Finally, there are certain formalities which need to be observed in the execution of these documents. After both the husband and wife-to-be sign the agreements, the original will be given to them. Copies will be given to each. These should be kept in safe places. The rabbi also keeps a copy.

In addition to all of the above, the following considerations ought to be kept in mind by both parties, when signing the prenuptial:

(1) The forms have been prepared for nationwide, as well as Canadian, use. Because in the U.S., marital disputes are decided under State law, each State has specific requirements for agreements which refer marital disputes to arbitration (e.g., number of witnesses, formalities of execution, signature of parties). To be on the safe side, we have proposed the use of two kosher witnesses and an acknowledgement in the manner appropriate for real estate transactions before a notary public. Before using these forms, which were specifically designed for use in New York, it would be wise to check with a competent local attorney who can suggest those formalities which are either necessary or desirable to comply with local law.

To avoid later disputes about whether the parties understood the agreements at the time they were executed, it would be prudent to let the parties study the agreements in advance, together with a fact sheet explaining the agreement, and to let each one decide whether to consult with their own attorney before signing the agreements. Since the interests of bride and groom are not identical, the rabbi should *not* suggest that they consult the same attorney. Whether or not either party actually consults with an attorney (or whether the couple jointly consults a single attorney) is less important than that each is advised that it may be desirable that each do so.

(2) The agreement offers a couple the option of referring questions of child custody and support to a *bet din* for decision. Couples should be told, however, that in no, or almost no, State will the secular courts defer to a *bet din* on matters of child custody. An agreement to arbitrate such disputes will give rise to expectations which cannot later be fulfilled.

(3) The prenuptial documents include a Hebrew version of the support obligation, patterned after the classical *tena'im,* as well as its English language equivalent. As a legal matter, it is preferable to utilize only the English version to avoid disputes concerning the accuracy of the translation and to dispel any question of whether the husband (or the wife) understands the nature of the document he or she is signing.

III
THE TEXT

Prenuptial Agreement

a. Husband's Assumption
of Obligation

I. I, the undersigned, _____,
husband-to-be, hereby obligate myself to support my wife-to-be, _____,
in the manner of Jewish husbands who feed
and support their wives loyally. If, God forbid,
we do not continue domestic residence together for whatever reason, then I now
(*me'achshav*) obligate myself to pay her $_____
per day, indexed annually to the Consumer
Price Index for all Urban Consumers (CPI-U)
as published by the US Department of Labor,
Bureau of Labor Statistics, beginning as of
December 31st following the date of our marriage, for food and support (*parnasah*) from
the day we no longer continue domestic residence together, and for the duration of our
Jewish marriage, which is payable each week

during the time due, under any circumstances, even if she has another source of income or earnings. Furthermore, I waive my *halakhic* rights to my wife's earnings for the period that she is entitled to the above-stipulated sum. However, this obligation (to provide food and support, *parnasah*) shall terminate if my wife refuses to appear upon due notice before the *Bet Din* of _____ or any other *bet din* specified in writing by that *bet din* before proceedings commence, for purpose of a hearing concerning any outstanding disputes between us, or in the event that she fails to abide by the decision or recommendation of such *bet din*.

II. I execute this document as an inducement to the marriage between myself and my wife-to-be. The obligations and conditions contained herein are executed according to all legal and *halakhic* requirements. I acknowledge that I have effected the above obligation by means of a *kinyan* (formal Jewish transaction) in an esteemed *(chashuv) bet din*.

III. I have been given the opportunity, prior to executing this document, of consulting with a rabbinic advisor and a legal advisor.

IV. I, the undersigned wife-to-be, acknowledge the acceptance of this obligation by my husband-to-be, and in partial reliance on it agree to enter into our forthcoming marriage.

Groom   Bride

Signature: Signature:
Name: Name:
Address: Address:

Signed at _____ Date_____

Witness_____ Witness _____

b. Arbitration Agreement between Husband and Wife

Memorandum of Agreement made this _____ day of _____ 57____, which is the _____ day of _____, 199_____, in the City of _____, State/Province of _____, between _____ the husband-to-be, who presently lives at _____ and the wife-to-be _____, who presently lives at _____. The parties are shortly going to be married.

I.   Should a dispute arise between the parties after they are married, Heaven forbid, so that they do not live together as husband and wife, they agree to refer their marital dispute to an arbitration panel, namely, the *Bet Din* of _____ for a binding decision. Each of the parties agrees to appear in person before the *bet din* at the demand of the other party.

II. The decision of the panel, or a majority of

them, shall be fully enforceable in any court of competent jurisdiction.

III. (a) The parties agree that the *bet din* is authorized to decide all issues relating to a *get* (Jewish divorce) as well as any issues arising from premarital agreements (e.g. *ketubah, tena'im*) entered into by the husband and the wife.

[The following three clauses (b,c,d) are optional, each to be separately included or excluded, by mutual consent, when signing this agreement.]

(b) The parties agree that the *bet din* is authorized to decide any other monetary disputes that may arise between them.

(c) The parties agree that the *bet din* is authorized to decide issues of child support, visitation and custody (if both parties consent to the inclusion of this provision in the arbitration at the time that the arbitration itself begins.)

(d) In deciding disputes pursuant to paragraph III b, the parties agree that the *bet din* shall apply the equitable distribution law of the State/Province of _____, as interpreted as of the date of this agreement, to any property disputes which may arise between them, the division of their property, and questions of support. Notwithstanding any other provision of the equitable distribution law, the *bet din* may take into account the respective responsibilities of the parties for the end of the marriage, as an additional, but not exclusive factor, in determining the distribution of marital property and support obligations.

IV. Failure of either party to perform his or her obligations under this agreement shall make that party liable for all costs awarded by either a *bet din* or a court of competent jurisdiction, including reasonable attorneys' fees, incurred by one side in order to obtain the other party's performance of the terms of this agreement.

V. (a) In the event any of the *bet din* members are unwilling or unable to serve, then their successors shall serve in their place. If there are no successors, the parties will at the time of the arbitration choose a mutually acceptable *bet din*. If no such *bet din* can be agreed upon, the parties shall each choose one member of the *bet din* and the two members selected in this way shall choose the third member. The decision of the *bet din* shall be made in accordance with Jewish Law (*halakhah*) and/or the general principles of arbitration and equity (*pesharah*) customarily employed by rabbinical tribunals.

(b) At any time, should there be a division of opinion among the members of the *bet din*, the decision of a majority of the members of the *bet din* shall be the decision of the *bet din*. Should any of the members of the *bet din* remain in doubt as to the proper decision, resign, withdraw, or refuse or become unable to perform duties, the remaining members shall render a decision. Their decision shall be that of the *bet din* for the purposes of this agreement.

(c) In the event of the failure of either party

to appear before it upon reasonable notice, the *bet din* may issue its decision despite the defaulting party's failure to appear.

VI. This agreement may be signed in one or more copies each one of which shall be considered an original.

VII. This agreement constitutes a fully enforceable arbitration agreement.

VIII.The parties acknowledge that each of them have been given the opportunity prior to signing this agreement to consult with their own rabbinic advisor and legal advisor.

In witness of all of the above, the Bride and Groom have entered into this agreement in the City of_____, State/Province of_____.

Groom   **Bride**

Signature: Signature:
Name: Name:
Address: Address:

Acknowledgements

State/Province of
County of   } ss.:
     On the_____ day of _____ 199__, before me personally came_____, the groom, to me known and known to me to be the indi-

vidual described in, and who executed the foregoing instrument, and duly acknowledged to me that
he executed the same.

_____
                        Notary Public

State/Province of
County of   } ss.:
      On the _____day of_____ 199__, before
me personally came _____, the bride, to me
known and known to me to be the individual described in, and who executed the foregoing instrument, and duly acknowledged to me that she executed the same.

_____
                 Notary Public

חתימת ידי תעיד עלי כמאה עדים שהתחייבתי
בקגא"ס לזון ולפרנס את אשתי מרת _____
כהלכות גוברין יהודאין דזנים ומפרנסים נשותיהם
בקושטא. ואם ח"ו לא מיתדר לנו לקבוע דירתנו
הקבועה ביחד בדירה אחת מאיזה טעם שיהיה, אני
מתחייב לה מעכשיו סך _____ דולר ליום עבור
מזונותיה ופרנסתה כל זמן היותנו נשואים כדת
משה וישראל. וחיוב מזונות ופרנסה בסך הנ"ל יהיה
בתוקפו גם אם יש לאשתי פרנסה ו\או הכנסה
ממקור אחר. ואני מוחל לה כל הזכויות והחיובים
שזוכה בהם אדם כשנושא אשה מתשמיש ומעשי
ידיה בזמן שחיוב סך הנ"ל בתוקפו. אולם אם
אזמין אותה לדין תורה בנידון הפירוד בב"ד _____
_____ וב"ד יפסקו עליה
שהיא לא צאית דינא בעניין הפירוד, הן משום
שתסרב להופיע לדין תורה, והן אם תבא לב"ד
והב"ד יפסקו ביניננו ואני אהיה מוכן לקיים פסק או
הצעת הב"ד והיא תסרב לקיים פסק או הצעת
הב"ד, יפסק חיובי זה. ואני מודה שההתחייבות
שבשטר זה נעשה בקנין המועיל בדין תורה וכחומר
כל שטרות בב"ד חשוב והתנאים נעשו כחומר כל
התנאים. ולראיה באתי על החתום ב _____ ימים
לחדש _____ שנת תש__ פה _____
והכל שריר וקים.
נאום _____

IV
PROMOTING THE PRENUPTIAL

Putting an End
to the *Agunah* Problem

Rabbi Basil Herring

We can call her Rachel. That is not her real name, but her story is real enough. When she married her husband, she thought she knew him well, but time proved otherwise. They lived together as husband and wife for one year, and had a child, before his physical abuse began. It took seven more years for her to finally receive the *get* that terminated the marriage. Seven years of emotional and physical pain, again and again approaching *batei din* and individual rabbis—including some genuinely concerned to assist; seven years running up lawyers' bills, threatening lawsuits, and even initiating public demonstrations. Seven wasted years that prevented both sides from remarrying or getting on with their lives, that required major financial

(reprinted with permission from *Amit Woman*, September 1994, pp. 17–21) outlays they could ill afford, and caused indelible scars not just for them, but for their child as well. In the end, Rachel still had to pay her husband a five-figure sum before he would agree to grant the *get*.

Why the recalcitrance? Simply because he refused to accept the notion that the marriage could not be saved.

Then there is the story of Leah (another pseudonym), whose 5 year battle centered on custody of their child. Even after her husband moved out, and she gave up her jewelry and their joint savings account, still he refused to give the *get*. When the judge granted her custody of their daughter (with visiting rights for her husband,) he bitterly castigated the husband for his refusal to cooperate with the court. The husband decided to use the *get* as leverage, till his demands for a better custody arrangement were met. Several *batei din* and hundreds of legal hours later, and only after severe synagogue and communal pressure, she finally received the *get*—principally because of an unusually sensitive *mesader gittin* (the rabbi who officiated at the *get* ceremony.)

THE PROBLEM

No one knows the numbers of current *agunot* (literally "chained women," Jewish women whose husbands cannot or will not grant them a *get*.) But with the rising rates of divorce in society at large reflected in the Jewish community, including the

Orthodox world, the *agunah* problem has taken on renewed urgency. Cases such as those described above have led many rabbis, community activists, and ordinary men and women to do something about the plight of such women.

It is not an easy task. The problem of recalcitrant spouses is one which has exercised Jewish communities over the generations. It arises from the fact that just as a halakhically valid marriage can only take place when both bride and groom participate willingly and without coercion, so too can the termination of marriage through divorce only take effect when both spouses consent freely to end the marriage. In Jewish law this is effected only through the voluntary granting by the husband of a *get* to his wife, who must willingly accept it. But given the anger or other difficulties often present when marriages break up, obtaining a *get* can easily become problematic, and in such cases the consequences for the individuals involved are dire indeed: a woman who remarries without the *get* is halakhically adulterous, and her children born thereafter are *mamzerim* (illegitimate,) forbidden by Jewish law to marry legitimate-born Jews. If a *mamzer* does, however, marry a legitimately born Jew, the children of this forbidden union are *mamzerim* as well, perpetuating the problem for generations. Thus such cases end up affecting the larger community as well.

Additionally, because of the current cultural climate in which many are quick to accuse laws and traditions such as ours of being biased against women, the issue of *agunot* is grist for the mill, and a source of tremendous *Chillul Hashem* (desecration of God's name,) easily magnified by the media.

Now, however, there seems to be a ray of light at the end of the tunnel. It is the prenuptial agreement formulated by Rabbi Mordechai Willig, a Rosh Yeshiva at Yeshiva University, and rabbi of the Young Israel of Riverdale, New York. This agreement was first suggested by Rabbi Zalman Nechemiah Goldberg of the Jerusalem Bet Din. It was then modified and endorsed by a number of leading *Rashei Bet Din* (heads of Rabbinical Courts) in America and Israel. They are Rabbi Ovadiah Yosef, the former Sephardic Chief Rabbi of Israel, now a member of the Supreme Rabbinical Court in Jerusalem, Rabbi Chaim Zimbalist of the Tel Aviv Bet Din, Rabbi Yitzchak Liebes, *Av Bet Din* of the Rabbinical Alliance of America, and Rabbi Gedalia Schwartz, head of the Beth Din of America, and of the Chicago Bet Din. The Rabbinical Council of America has urged its members to use the agreement in every wedding ceremony at which they officiate.

THE AGREEMENT

The document in question, a prenuptial agreement to be signed by both husband- and wife-to-be, effectively says that the husband agrees to continue to maintain and support his wife until such time as the marriage is properly terminated. A particular sum for this support is stipulated, approximating the actual cost of living for this couple, at the time of the marriage (currently $100 per day for the average couple, but in all cases to be adjusted in accordance with financial circumstances,) and indexed for future fluctuations in the cost of living. Thus, should the time come when the couple no longer lives together as husband and wife, the husband will have significant incentive to give the *get,* and will be unable to claim that it is a *get me'useh* (or forced *get,* which is halakhically invalid) insofar as he has the alternative of maintaining the wife at the agreed-upon sum.

Yet the husbands too are protected by the agreement. If the wife refuses to appear upon due notice before a *bet din* to rule on any outstanding disputes between them, or if she fails to abide by the decision or recommendation of the *bet din*, then the husband's obligation is terminated.

A second document, signed by both parties at the time of marriage, stipulates that in case of disagreement at the time of a future breakup, they agree to have their dispute adjudicated by a specified *bet din*, acceptable to both parties. This second document minimizes the likelihood of either spouse unfairly exploiting the terms of the prenuptial, or putting up the kind of procedural roadblocks which are today unfortunately all too common in such cases. It also allows for any unforeseen circumstances to be handled in a fair and equitable manner.

An important issue concerning the prenuptial approach to the *agunah* problem is its enforceability in secular courts. In the United States, for example, courts are generally loathe to interfere in

religious practices or disputes because of the constitutional separation between church and state.
Thus some have raised the question of whether the
prenuptial agreement will be upheld in secular
courts as a binding contract if either party refuses
to abide by the terms of the agreement (i.e., the
payment stipulated) or to accede to the ruling of
the designated *bet din*. While it is true that the prenuptial has not to date been tested in the courts,
the prenuptial addresses this issue in its English
formulation. A number of subsequent emenda-
tions and refinements have been incorporated
into the prenuptial since the original document
was formulated, taking into consideration the various legal and constitutional issues involved. This
includes an optional clause invoking the principle
of equitable distribution of marital assets. Of
course the fine print may vary, depending on the
state or country involved.

STANDARDIZING THE AGREEMENT

Doubtless there are some couples who might re-
coil at the prospect of considering—let alone signing—such a document just prior to marriage, when
love, good faith, and mutual trust, are uppermost
in their minds. To inject such unpleasant thoughts
and provisions into so joyous a time seems awk-
ward. Yet the *ketubah* which is signed at every Orthodox wedding, in fact does precisely this. In a
time-honored Aramaic formulation, it addresses

the possibility of death and divorce and their financial consequences—albeit implicitly. Indeed, this type of prenuptial agreement is found in the classical *tena'im,* the standardized contract between Jewish husbands and wives. Furthermore, by signing the agreement, today's bride and groom are in fact clearly stating their commitment to each other's happiness and well-being, no matter what the future may bring.

These are strong arguments in favor of incorporating the prenuptial agreement into all Jewish marriage procedures. But strongest of all is the consideration that only if all, or most, marrying couples sign such a prenuptial, will its true deterrent effect take hold. Thus, even if a couple were convinced that their spouses-to-be would never withhold a *get*—something which experience has taught can never be certain, in the absence of prophecy—it would be important for them to sign it nonetheless, as an act of social conscience and Judaic responsibility. In this light, the refusal to sign a prenuptial could well be viewed as indicative of a character flaw, a lack of flexibility, or at the very least an insensitivity to the needs of others. Moreover the standardization of this practice throughout the rabbinate would successfully remove the onus of social stigma from individual couples signing prenuptial agreements. The couples could merely state that "we wanted Rabbi X to officiate at our wedding, and he makes *everybody* sign it."

The prenuptial agreement will not solve all *agunah* problems. And it can only help those who sign it; those who marry or have married without signing such an agreement will not benefit directly from its provisions. But as it become more and more accepted, with the help of God, we can hope that the very idea of using a *get* for ulterior motives, no matter what the justification, and irrespective of whatever may have preceded the marital breakup, will become less and less tolerated by the Jewish community. This is especially true for the Orthodox community, which is the one that, in the end, suffers the most from this terrible injustice.

As Rabbi Saul Berman has written, in urging rabbinic implementation of the prenuptial agreement, "we only rarely have the opportunity to shape a new and universal practice while simultaneously helping to prevent Jewish immorality. Such a joint opportunity is now before us. Our creativity can mold the practice, our capacity as teachers and leaders will be tested in the process of convincing this coming first generation of users to be comfortable with the process, and our ethical vigor will leave a lasting mark on all future generations of Jews." But rabbis alone cannot achieve this transformation. All too often, rabbis who try to have the agreement signed by prospective brides and grooms report that the very newness of the concept is a major obstacle.

It behooves us all to do what we can to change this attitude. Here, as elsewhere in contemporary Jewish life, we need to forge a sacred partnership involving rabbis *and* laypersons, men *and* women, the single *and* the married, parents *and* adult children, to ensure that the scourge of the *agunah*, with its attendant religious and social pathologies, and its immense potential for human suffering, is relegated forever to the past.

Pastoral Considerations in the Presentation of the Prenuptial Agreement

Rabbi Robert Hirt,
Rabbi Haskel Lookstein,
Rabbi Abner Weiss,
and Rabbi Jeffrey R. Woolf

THE DIFFICULTY IN RAISING THE SUBJECT

It might appear strange and inappropriate that, during the course of a premarital counselling session, a rabbi should raise the specter of divorce so as to advocate the use of a prenuptial agreement. No wonder some rabbis' first reaction is to avoid the subject altogether. After all, at a time filled with anticipation of marital bliss, precisely when the two young people before him are deeply in love, why should the rabbi be the one to turn their attention to a scenario in which their marriage may fail and dissolve? Yet in spite of the discomfort, and the momentary unpleasantness, it might well be that by raising the subject in an appropriate time and fashion, the rabbi fulfills his highest obligation to the couple before him, in a spirit, paradoxically, of *hava'at shalom bein adam le'chaveiro*, i.e., cultivating peace, and conflict avoidance, between his fellow men. For the signing of a prenuptial agreement, sensitively and effectively done, might well avoid endless grief and suffering for that couple in years to come, if, God forbid, the marriage does dissolve, in rancor or animosity.

HOW TO RAISE THE MATTER

How then is a rabbi to introduce this admittedly difficult subject? The concept of the prenuptial agreement should be presented at the first premarital conference with the rabbi, preferably toward its conclusion. This will allow a gradual development of trust and empathy between the rabbi and the couple, essential to the effective presentation of the premarital agreement. During the early part of the conference, the rabbi should convey to the couple that he recognizes how deeply they love and respect each other, and that he has every confidence that their marriage will be successful, life-long, and a source of great happiness to them, their families, and, God willing, their future children. Having so assured the couple, he can then introduce the matter of a prenuptial agreement.

TWO APPROACHES

At that point, two possible approaches can be utilized by the rabbi. One possibility favored by some rabbis, is to deliberately distance the couple from the harsher implications of the agreement. It could be explained that this is a touchy subject, one that is not intended for them personally, but rather as a method of dealing with a very difficult communal problem. The problem ought to be explained in terms of how many women—and sometimes men—are subjected to extortion for all kinds of reasons, without being able to receive a religious divorce after a civil divorce has been given. The rabbi then explains that leading halakhic authorities and heads of *batei din* have in recent years drafted a particular agreement that has received widespread approval in the Orthodox community. It is a document that possesses the potential to solve the problem, if only it would be used by every engaged couple. Their signing of this agreement thus serves as an expression of their sense of communal responsibility for all Jewish couples, and particularly for Jewish women. They are urged to make this commitment to the entire Jewish people specifically at a time that they are undertaking to build a *bayit ne'eman be'Yisrael.*

An alternate approach might address these harsher implications directly. The document could be presented as an expression of love and concern for one another. The rabbi could ask the young man and woman whether they love one another. Expectedly, the couple would most likely protest that they are marrying each other precisely because they love each other and wish to live as husband and wife, establishing a new Jewish family. This type of response can cue the rabbi to ask, if so, whether they would knowingly hurt each another. Given the (again) expected protestations of "certainly not," the rabbi can ask whether either of them have heard of the *agunah* problem in its contemporary context. Whether they have or not, the rabbi should then describe the requirement of Jewish law that a *get* be executed by mutual consent. He should make the point that this is the most civilized way of dissolving a relationship which has not worked. However this does not always work in practice. In practice, both husband and wife are vulnerable to the manipulations of an angry, greedy or malicious partner. The husband can refuse to execute a *get,* leaving his wife an *agunah.* The wife can refuse to receive a *get,* which in most instances prevents the husband from re-marrying. In some cases, one side (usually the husband) stoops to outright extortion of money or leverage on the divorce settlement as the "price" for executing or receiving a *get.*

THE PRENUPTIAL AND OTHER HALAKHIC DOCUMENTS

In either case, at this point of the discussion, the rabbi should draw the couple's attention to the fact that this document has significant precedent. He should point out that the *ketubah* itself is a pre-marital agreement, protecting the wife in the event of the death of the husband or of divorce, by guaranteeing her a significant sum of money. Until recently, moreover, other detailed obligations between prospective spouses were incorporated in a document known as *tena'im*. Some of these, in fact, reflected some of the very concerns which have been raised by the rabbi.

The rabbi should then review the document with the couple and explain its halakhic and legal bases to them. They should be encouraged to ask as many questions as they wish, and to seek the advice of their attorneys before signing, at the next premarital conference. This could provide the opportunity for a discussion of relationships and strategies for the resolution of marital (and perhaps, engagement) conflicts and stresses. This discussion would, most likely, continue on into the next session.

CONCLUSION

Which ever approach is adopted, the key on the part of the rabbi is to present marriage and family life as a joyous, trusting and love-filled experience—that nonetheless require realism and reasonable expectations and precautions, be it for oneself, or for the benefit of the Jewish community at large and future generations of Jews. So approached, the signing of a prenuptial can become a profound and integral link in the continuity and sanctity of marriage.

Sample Rabbinic Letter
to a Bridal Couple

Dear (Bride and Groom,)

Mazel tov again, on your forthcoming wedding. I am looking forward to it with great anticipation of what will, I am sure, be a wonderful *simchah.*

I am writing to you (as I do to all bridal couples) to raise what I consider an important matter for your future happiness: the signing of a prenuptial agreement. When we will meet to discuss marriage, family life, and the details of the wedding ceremony, we will discuss the matter further, but for now I'd like to touch on the benefits of having such an agreement between the two of you. As a matter of fact the Rabbinical Council of America has urged all its members not to officiate at a marriage unless a prenuptial has been signed, for the simple reason that it is so obviously in the interest of both the bride and groom. A copy of the agreement is enclosed with this letter, for you to examine at your leisure.

What exactly is involved in this agreement?

You may have read or heard reports of women (and sometimes, although rarely, men too) who find themselves in the position of an *agunah*. That is to say that if their marriage has broken up, and a civil divorce has been granted, they cannot remarry for many years, if ever, because they have not had a religious divorce (known as a *get*, given by the husband to the wife, in the presence of a rabbinical court.) There are today thousands of Jewish women who find themselves in that situation, because their husbands (perhaps out of anger, or spite, or to gain custody, or for whatever reason) refuse to initiate the *get*, as required by Jewish law. Even for men, remarriage is extremely difficult, if the wife for whatever reason refuses to receive a *get* from him. Unfortunately there is no way a husband or a wife can be forced to give or receive a *get*–for it must be voluntarily undertaken to be valid. Thus some women or men might find themselves or their families subject to blackmail or other injustices, as their spouse withholds the *get* for ulterior motive. And experience has taught that there is no sure way of knowing which marriage this might happen to, no matter how much the groom and bride love and respect each other prior to marriage.

In response to this situation (and I might say, as well, to demands by women's groups that something be done about it,) leading orthodox rabbis, together with some respected legal scholars, have devised the enclosed prenuptial agreement to be signed by both bride and groom before the wedding takes place. Essentially it says that in the unlikely case that the marriage fails, the husband agrees that he will continue to maintain and support the wife on a daily basis until he gives, and she receives, a *get*, assuming she too complies with the proper requirements expected of her. A second agreement, attached to the first, stipulates that in case of a dispute as to the implementation of the agreement, they agree to binding arbitration before a specifically named rabbinical court. These agreements are carefully worded, based on rabbinic and legal experience and requirements; they encourage the signers to consult with their own rabbi and lawyer if they have any questions; and they can be tailored to the specific needs of the couple. The bottom line is that they give strong incentive to expedite a *get*, and thereby prevent some future injustice, for either the wife or husband.

Please read the agreement in both its parts carefully; discuss it with each other and others whose opinion you value. By signing it you will not be implying any less love for the one you now love so much—but in fact you will demonstrate your selfless concern for each other, no matter what the future will bring.

I have every reason to expect that yours will be a long and wonderful marriage, blessed by God in every way, for you are a very special couple. At the same time, however, I urge you to agree to sign the prenuptial, and in so doing to help not only yourselves, but the Jewish community here and around the world eliminate this problem once and for all.

Again, mazeltov—with best wishes for a loving, caring, and beautiful marriage.

Sincerely,

(Rabbi)

The Authors

(in alphabetical order)

Rabbi Kenneth Auman is the rabbi of the Young Israel of Flatbush, NY.

Rabbi Saul Berman is on the faculty of Stern College for Women, at Yeshiva University.

Rabbi Basil Herring is the rabbi of the Jewish Center of Atlantic Beach, NY, and is the Coordinator of the Orthodox Caucus.

Rabbi Robert Hirt is the Vice-President for Administration and Professional Education of RIETS at Yeshiva University

Dr. Norman Lamm is the President of Yeshiva University.

Rabbi Haskel Lookstein is the rabbi of Congregation Kehillath Jeshurun, NY.

Rabbi Gedalia Dov Schwartz is the Rosh Beth Din of the Beth Din of America.

Marc Stern is Co-director of the Commission on Law and Social Action, the American Jewish Congress.

Rabbi Avraham Weiss is the rabbi of the Hebrew Institute of Riverdale, NY, and is on the faculty of Stern College for Women at Yeshiva University.

Rabbi Abner Weiss is the rabbi of Beth Jacob Congregation, Beverly Hills, CA.

Rabbi Mordechai Willig is the rabbi of the Young Israel of Riverdale, and a Rosh Yeshiva at RIETS, Yeshiva University.

Rabbi Jeffrey R. Woolf is on the faculty of Bar Ilan University, and is a past Coordinator of the Orthodox Caucus.